Putting the Brakes
on Car Crime

First published in 1993 by
The Children's Society   and   Mid Glamorgan Social Services Dept
Edward Rudolf House   Greyfriars Road
Margery Street   Cardiff
London WC1X 0JL   South Glamorgan

A catalogue record for this book is available from the British Library.

ISBN 0 907324 83 5

Cover design: Jan Brown

Printed by: Nuffield Press

Putting the brakes on car crime

A local study of auto-related crime among young people

Maureen McGillivray
Wales Advocacy Unit

Authors: Maureen McGillivray, Wales Advocacy Unit,
The Children's Society

Anne Crowley, Wales Advocacy Unit,
The Children's Society

Howell Edwards, Principal Officer,
Mid Glamorgan Social Services

MID GLAMORGAN
COUNTY COUNCIL · CYNGOR SIR
MORGANNWG GANOL

The Children's Society
MAKING LIVES WORTH LIVING
A VOLUNTARY SOCIETY OF THE CHURCH OF ENGLAND AND THE CHURCH IN WALES

Contents

PART I

INTRODUCTION

Background

Car crime — a growing problem

The 1980s and 90s have witnessed a dramatic increase in crime involving motor vehicles. The statistics are alarming. From April 1991 to March 1992 in England and Wales, 5.4 million notifiable offences were recorded by the police, an increase of 700,000 offences (15%) over the previous year. Car crime accounted for one-quarter of this increase, with 1.5 million offences, equivalent to 28% of all recorded crime.

Of the 1.5 million car crime incidents, 17% were thefts from a vehicle and 11% thefts of a vehicle. Thefts of vehicles have risen by 50% between 1989 and 1993, thefts from vehicles by 56%. From April 1991 to March 1992 the clear-up rate[1] for theft from a vehicle was only 19%; for theft of a vehicle, the rate was 24%.

It is estimated by the Association of British Insurers that, on average, a car in Britain is broken into, stolen or vandalized every 25 seconds and that a stolen car is 200 times more likely to be involved in an accident than one driven by its owner. This has resulted in massively increased insurance premiums.

[1]An offence is regarded as cleared up if a person has been charged, summonsed or cautioned for the offence, or the offence has been admitted and is to be taken into consideration by the court.

1

Car break-ins result in £193 million of insurance claims each year. The financial cost of stolen cars is estimated to be at least £1.2 billion each year, of which £500 million is taken up in insurance costs and the rest in criminal justice costs. The human cost is, of course, impossible to calculate.

The statistics indicate that a high proportion of thefts of and from cars are committed by young offenders. In 1990, 78% of those found guilty or cautioned for theft of and from cars were between 10 and 20 years old; 40% were aged between 10 and 16. Although statistics relating to all types of offending behaviour indicate that there has been a 37% decline in the total number of known juvenile offenders (under 17 years old) since 1985, it appears that car crime has become an increasingly popular activity amongst this population.

Previous studies (see Appendix 1) have indicated that car theft can provide a degree of excitement and status for young people otherwise disaffected. Light et al. (1993) suggest that excessive levels of car theft are akin to adolescent infatuation or obsession.

The high level of media attention which has been focused on the incidence of young people driving powerful cars at great speed and a number of fatal accidents involving young drivers in stolen vehicles have fuelled understandable public concern and calls for effective action.

Tackling car crime in South Wales

The need for effective and integrated policies to deal with the increasing problem of car crime among young people in South Wales led, in 1991, to the setting up by the South Wales Juvenile and Young Persons Committee of an Auto-Crime Standing Committee. This is a multi-agency initiative involving Social Services, Probation and the Police from the three Glamorgan local authorities.

A report published by the Standing Committee in 1991 (*A Practical Approach to Auto-Crime*) highlighted the extent of the problem in South Wales. In 1990, for example, 20,141 vehicles were taken without their owner's consent, which represented an increase of 20% on the previous year.

In November 1992, the Committee organized a national conference, drawing together representatives from a wide range of relevant agencies from all parts of the United Kingdom. The conference was used to launch the publication of a Policy Discussion Document, *Tackling Car Crime — The Positive Approach*. This document proposed that any car crime strategy should include three elements:

1. Crime Prevention schemes
2. Education programmes
3. Programmes of work with known offenders

Following the conference, county-based working parties were established with the task of producing draft strategies for dealing with car crime.

The Working Party established in Mid Glamorgan included representatives from both the statutory and the voluntary sectors. The brief of this Working Party was to outline a Car Crime Strategy for Mid Glamorgan which would be presented to the South Wales Juvenile and Young Peoples Committee by the end of March 1993. It would also be used as a focus for discussion with relevant agencies.

A pre-requisite for any attempt to combat a problem is a full assessment and understanding of that problem. Despite increasing public concern, there is, as Light et al. (1993) note, "a relative scarcity of significant work on the subject [of car crime]". (Previous research is reviewed in Appendix 1.)

In January 1992, in anticipation of the formation of the Working Party, Mid Glamorgan Social Services therefore commissioned the Wales Advocacy Unit of The Children's Society to produce an independent report on the extent of car crime involving young people in the area and to suggest possible ways forward. Reflecting increasing public concern, it was requested that the study place particular emphasis on young people's involvement in the offence of 'Taking (a vehicle) Without the Owner's Consent' (TWOC), or 'joyriding', as it is often inappropriately called.

The report was published in February 1993 and has acted as a cornerstone for the deliberations of the Working Party. The current report presents findings of national interest arising from The Children's Society's original study, together with Mid Glamorgan Social Services Department's subsequent response.

3

Introduction

A national perspective

Despite the size of the problem, little work has been done to assess the nature of young people's involvement in car crime and tailor a response accordingly. Why are some young people increasingly risking their own and other people's lives, as they drive around in stolen cars? What can be done to stop it?

Increasingly, courts and local authorities are acknowledging that custodial sentences fail to prevent re-offending. Statistics showing re-offending rates as high as 100% (Isles, 1992), together with anecdotal evidence suggests that for some young people, stealing cars has become a true addiction.

This report outlines a unique attempt to develop a strategy to combat car crime by first attempting to understand the problem in a local context. The findings, particularly the recurrent themes that emerge, will be of interest to others seeking to address the problem in different parts of the country. The study itself and Mid-Glamorgan's response provide a helpful example of what can be done on a local level. Thus, it is hoped that the report will contribute to the development of more effective strategies for tackling car crime throughout the country.

Research design, methodology and report structure

The objectives of the study by The Children's Society were to:

- examine the incidence and nature of car crime amongst juveniles (under-17-year-olds) in Mid Glamorgan;
- suggest ways forward to reduce the incidence of car crime in the area.

In order to meet these objectives, the research design used a variety of data collection methods to obtain both quantitative and qualitative information.

Methodology

i) Police records were examined to assess the extent and nature of the problem in the area. We acknowledge that with regard to crime in general, such records underestimate the real picture: *The British Crime Survey, 1989* suggests that only 41 out of every 100 offences committed are reported to the police and only 26 out of 100 are recorded by the police.

The disparity between official records and actual levels of car crime is, however, less stark. Crime incidents involving vehicles are more frequently reported to the police in order to facilitate insurance claims. Thus, it was felt that the police records provide the best available information relating to a large number of car crime incidents in the area.

ii) Semi-structured interviews were conducted with 17 young people who were or had been involved in stealing cars. Sixteen were male, one was female. The interviews addressed particular topics (see Appendix 3) concerned with the nature of car theft, the young people's motivation, and possible deterrents. These interviews provided a depth and breadth of information unobtainable from records.

iii) Interviews were also conducted with specialist social workers to ascertain their views on the extent and nature of car crime among young people in their area. A limited review of existing Social Services provision aimed at managing the problem was conducted and respondents were asked what they would do to tackle the problem if they had unlimited resources and power. Similar issues were addressed in a small postal survey of police officers.

iv) A limited review of existing research was also undertaken, including any evaluations of current iniatives focusing on car crime.

Structure of the report

Having so far attempted in Part One of this report to set the issue of car crime within a national perspective and to outline the events and process leading to the writing of the report, this section concludes with a brief summary of car crime from a legal perspective.

Part Two presents the main findings of The Children's Society's research into car crime involving young people in Mid Glamorgan, beginning with a short profile of the county. Analysis of data collated from Police Juvenile Records is followed by the findings from the semi-structured interviews with young people, which provide an insight into the complexities of car crime and the motivations of those who become involved.

Part Three analyses a range of responses to car crime, including those of the courts, crime prevention initiatives and media coverage. In particular, the potential of motor projects is assessed.

Based on the findings of the report, Part Four offers a series of recommendations for ways forward for those seeking to develop strategies to address car crime. This section includes a case example of the work of the Mid Glamorgan Car Crime Working Party, a summary of the information collated on initiatives already in existence in the county, the main conclusions of the proposed Car Crime Strategy for Mid Glamorgan, and subsequent developments.

Finally, appendices present an evaluation of existing research, a summary of the law and penalties relating to car crime offences, and a list of the questions used as the basis for the semi-structured interviews with young people.

What constitutes car crime?
—legal definitions

An ever-growing and increasingly complex legal framework has developed in response to the extent and nature of car crime offences being committed. (Appendix 2 contains details of the way in which the law is applied to cases of car theft.)

One early example of the way in which legislation has had to be reviewed and revised over the years in order to cover 'new' aspects of improper behaviour, is the Road Traffic Act 1930. This introduced the concept of 'taking and driving away', as previously offenders could only be charged with stealing petrol.

Under current legislation, for a charge of theft to be brought, it has to be proved that there was an intention to permanently deprive. This would mean, for example, selling the vehicle, changing the number plates or causing irreparable damage. The offence of TWOC (taking without owner's consent) was introduced in the Theft Act 1968, due to the difficulty of proving an intention to permanently deprive. The offence was triable either in the Crown Court or the Magistrate's Court, until the Criminal Justice Act 1988 made it an offence triable on summary conviction only i.e. in the Magistrates' Court only.

Legislation covering car theft has come under criticism from those working within the criminal justice system. Some believe that enforced jurisdication in the lower courts for TWOC has encouraged a perception that car theft is not viewed as a very serious offence and will therefore not attract stiff penalties. They argue that this has contributed significantly to the huge increase in car theft. This view is firmly based on the assumption that 'stiff penalties' are an effective deterrent.

No doubt this thinking contributed to the introduction of the Aggravated Vehicle-Taking Act in April 1992, which increases the courts' powers for imposing custodial sentences on car thieves. Under the Act, a person has first to be found guilty of the basic offence of taking a vehicle. They will be guilty of an additional aggravated offence and liable to more serious penalties if: they drive dangerously; they cause injury or death; or they cause damage to the vehicle or other property.

The maximum penalty is two years imprisonment, or five years if death is caused. There is also an unlimited fine and an automatic driving ban.

PART II

THE LOCAL STUDY

Profile of Mid Glamorgan

Mid Glamorgan has a population of approximately 550,000, the largest of any county in Wales. Rapid industrial decline, particularly in coal mining, has left it one of the most deprived areas in Britain.

The Economic Policy and Research Unit of Mid Glamorgan compared Mid Glamorgan with other counties in Wales in 1991 and found it had the highest rate of: unemployed men, women and young people; school leavers without qualifications; households with no savings; households without a car; crime; death. It was also found to have the poorest housing stock in Wales.

In 1992, Mid Glamorgan Social Crime Prevention Unit carried out a survey of more than 13,000 young people attending school in Mid Glamorgan, aged between 13 and 18 years. The questionnaire investigated issues of crime, alcohol, drugs and leisure. The Crime Prevention Unit's findings (unpublished) make the point that the responses to the survey need to be seen in the "context of the poverty and lack of confidence in the future that prevailed".

The findings provide useful background information to the study of car crime. They confirm, for example, the importance of peer group pressure. The young people surveyed spent 68% of their spare time with friends and only 27% with their family. They were also asked how they spent their leisure time. Almost one in five (60%) said their favourite activity was "hanging around the streets".

The Local Study

A number of questions were also asked about alcohol and drugs. Of the total sample, 94% had drunk alcohol. Of these, 94% were aged 15 or younger. Of all 13-year-olds, 36% had drunk in the week prior to the survey. During the previous week, 10% of all those questioned had used drugs. The proportion who had been offered drugs was 32%.

The questionnaire asked the young people about any crimes they had committed, including any that had gone undetected. Three per cent of respondents admitted stealing a car or a motorbike. Males were almost six times more likely to commit this offence than females. Theft from cars was admitted by 6% of all respondents, while 16% admitted damaging a car.

The reasons given for committing these crimes and others were: 'boredom' (49%), 'for money' (44%), 'encouraged/dared by friends' (43%), 'didn't think I'd be caught' (36%) and 'had been drinking' (35%).

The majority (75%) had been to a youth club once but only 18% became regular attenders. The young people identified some facilities they would like to be able to use in youth clubs. These were: video games (85%), non-alcoholic bar (82%), and coffee bar (81%). The majority (56%) also wanted more sporting facilities.

Car crime in Mid Glamorgan: data from Police Juvenile Crime Reports, April 1991– March 1992

In order to focus on information concerning the incidence of car crime amongst young people, it was necessary to obtain data from the Police Juvenile Crime Reports forms. These contain details of the offence, the young person charged and whether or not the offence(s) is denied or admitted. They are used to report an incident to a multi-agency consultative process.

As is common practice throughout England and Wales, South Wales Police consult with representatives of the welfare agencies, i.e. Social Services, Probation and Education, as to what course of action to take regarding a juvenile charged with an offence. In cases where the offence is admitted, the decision focuses primarily on whether to caution or to prosecute the young offender.

Data from 2577 Juvenile Crime Reports was studied.

This method of data collection has limitations: as previously mentioned, only a proportion of crime is actually recorded by the police; police forms are processed for all incidents, including those where young people deny the offence for which they have been charged; some information was not always recorded, for example, details of the consultative process recommendation and the final outcome. As a result, and with the collection instruments available, it proved impossible to assess how juvenile car thieves were dealt with within the local justice system.

The Local Study

Recorded level of car crime for which juveniles were charged:
Car crime represented 18% of all crime processed through the pre-court juvenile consultative process between April 1991 and March 1992.

The most common car crime offence recorded was taking without owner's consent (TWOC), which accounted for 42%, followed by theft of a vehicle (29%), and being carried (17%). Although the number of incidents of theft from vehicles was noted in total (4%), no further information was gathered about that type of offence nor about the young person involved. The remaining 9% of recorded incidents involved charges of tampering with a vehicle, going equipped to steal and attempted theft. Again, no further information was gathered with regard to this miscelleanous category.

Time of year, time of day and place of offence:
The month of the offence was noted to determine if there was any seasonal variation over the year. The number of offences in April 1991 was 41 and remained relatively constant at around 30 per month from May to August; it rose in September (37), before slumping to a low in December (9), then rising to reach its highest in March 1992 (48).

Figure 1
Level of car crime each month from April 1991 to March 1992

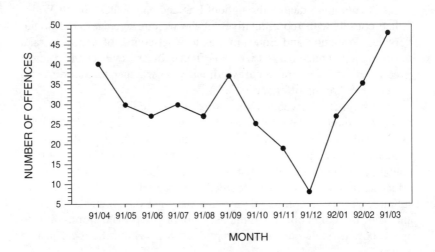

12

The time of the offence was not always recorded (35% were unrecorded). Of the offences recorded, there were certain peak times when more cars were stolen. They were 8pm, 9pm and 11pm. The main period of inactivity appears to be between 6am and 8am.

Figure 2
Times when car crimes were committted

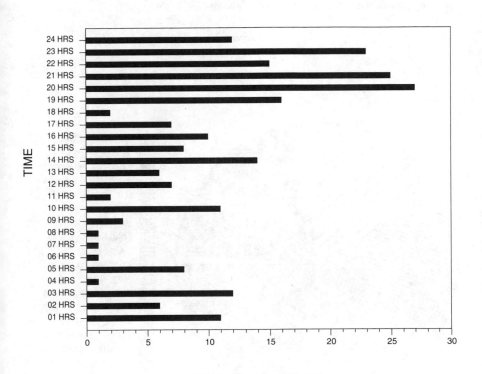

■ Number of vehicles taken

Incident committed jointly or alone:
Records indicated that 81% of crimes were committed jointly, 11% were committed alone and in 8% of cases the information was not recorded on the police form.

Type of vehicle stolen:
In 35% of the cases, no make of vehicle was specified on the police forms. Motor cycles accounted for 18% of vehicles stolen. Of the remaining 47%, figure 3 below shows the make and model of vehicles stolen. Cases where no model of vehicle was recorded are shown separately under the general category of the make of vehicle (eg. Vauxhall or Ford).

Figure 3
Type of vehicle stolen

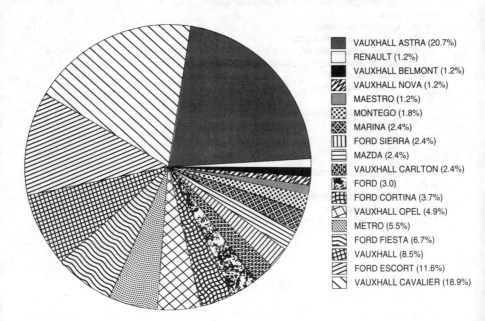

- VAUXHALL ASTRA (20.7%)
- RENAULT (1.2%)
- VAUXHALL BELMONT (1.2%)
- VAUXHALL NOVA (1.2%)
- MAESTRO (1.2%)
- MONTEGO (1.8%)
- MARINA (2.4%)
- FORD SIERRA (2.4%)
- MAZDA (2.4%)
- VAUXHALL CARLTON (2.4%)
- FORD (3.0)
- FORD CORTINA (3.7%)
- VAUXHALL OPEL (4.9%)
- METRO (5.5%)
- FORD FIESTA (6.7%)
- VAUXHALL (8.5%)
- FORD ESCORT (11.6%)
- VAUXHALL CAVALIER (18.9%)

Details of the young person charged

Gender:
All previous research has shown that car crime is mainly committed by males (a fact that seems to have been largely ignored or taken for granted by policy makers). In Mid Glamorgan during the period of study, 92% of young people charged with car theft were male. Of the 8% of females charged, 68% were arrested for 'being carried' in a stolen vehicle.

Age:
The majority of young people charged with car theft offences were 15 or 16 years old (69%). The youngest age recorded was 11 years.

Figure 4.
Type of offence committed by each age group

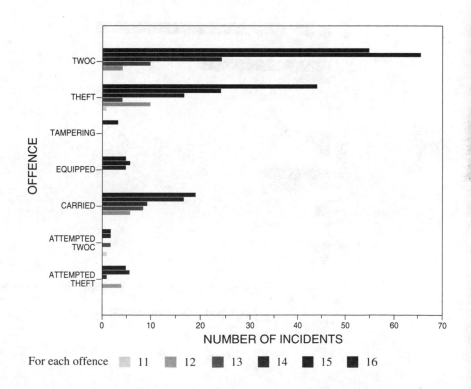

15

Accommodated by the local authority:

The records indicated that at the time of offence, 25% of those charged were looked after by the local authority. In 6% of cases, no information was recorded.

Previous convictions of young people:

In 19% of cases, it was not known whether the young person had any previous convictions. In the remainder of cases, 58% of the young people had previous convictions, 23% did not.

Figure 5 below shows how many of the young people had previous convictions by category of the current alleged offence.

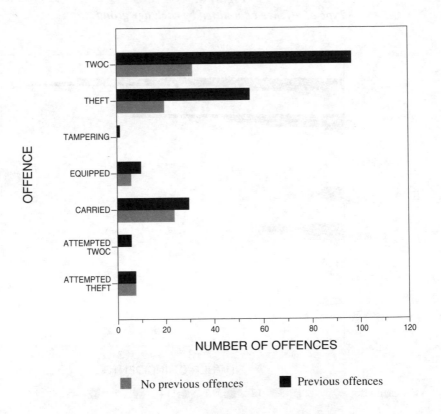

Figure 5
Previous convictions for each offence

Interviews with young people

The interviews with the young people generated a wealth of valuable data demonstrating the complexity of the issues. Seventeen young people were identified by Social Services for interview. The sample aimed to reflect a cross-section of those involved in car crime in the area. Some had only been involved for a short time, others had a long career of offending. Of the 17 interviewed, only one young person was female. Although she had never stolen a car, she had been carried as a passenger. Her responses were included, where possible, in the final analysis.

Although the sample was small, due in large part to the timescale of the research, a large amount of data was gathered and general themes began to emerge. The young people's responses have been analysed under the following headings:

1. Initial involvement in car crime
2. Extent of a sub-culture
3. Process of taking a car
4. Types of cars taken
5. Time of day
6. Locations from which cars are taken
7. Driving
8. Car chases
9. Theft from cars
10. Motivation
11. Deterrents
12. Consequences

The 17 young people came from a variety of backgrounds. All had been in care, placed either on a voluntary basis, for welfare reasons or for their offending. All had been found guilty or cautioned of other types of offences as well as car theft.

Many of the young people had been in the same care institution together and knew each other either personally or by reputation. At least three were known to use drugs and one of the sample said he committed offences to finance his drug-taking.

The interviews were semi-structured and lasted for approximately one hour. A copy of the questionnaire used as the basis for the interviews is included in Appendix 3.

Table 1 below shows the age of each of the 17 young people at the time of interview, the age at which they said they began taking cars, and their estimate of how many cars they had stolen.

Table 1

Young person's age at time of interview	Age when started	Approximate number of cars taken
12	10	20
15	12	50–100
15	12	500
15	12	100s
16	13	100s
16	13	50–100
16	14	50+
16	14	50+
16	15	20
16	15	carried
16	15	2
16	15	100+
16	16	20
17	12	300–400
17	14	15
17	15	50–70
17	15	200

Average age of those interviewed: 15.8
Average age when started: 13.6

1. INITIAL INVOLVEMENT IN CAR CRIME

The young people's first involvement with taking cars showed it to be an activity carried out with others and influenced by peer group pressure.

All those interviewed stated that they were with others the first time they were involved with taking cars. A number were passengers only, while others were 'bored' and started checking car doors and windows when they were out. One person said he watched his friends take cars for three months before he took one himself.

All those questioned had learnt how to get into cars by watching others.

> *"I helped people to take them but didn't learn to drive for two years. I was a passenger 'til then."*

Most said they had learnt to drive by watching either their friends or members of their family. One person said he only chose automatic cars at first until his confidence grew. Another said his father had taught him when he was 11 and commented, "He didn't think I'd nick cars though."

All but one of those interviewed said driving was quite easy, and most had started driving for the first time on roads, although a few had started on waste ground or in fields. One person said he had bought his own car and taught himself to drive on an old railway line.

One respondent described his first time behind the wheel of a car as follows:

> *"The first time, I smashed it up. I'd been watching and I thought it would be no trouble to drive, I knew where every-thing was. I was crunching the gears — I knew what they were and how to use them but they were chunky and then I got con-fused when I saw other things coming towards me, I forgot to do things."*

2. EXTENT OF A SUB-CULTURE

A series of questions was asked to ascertain the extent of any sub-culture. There appeared to be an established network for passing on knowledge about how to take cars. Each group would have their own rules: for example, they would never burn out a car after they had finished with it

19

even though they knew other groups or gangs who did. Some seemed to take pride in doing as little damage as possible to a car. Although they all admitted they were doing wrong, in their eyes it was 'justified' as the owners would get their cars back later with very little damage or be compensated by their insurance company.

All of the respondents said they had friends who took cars. One young person qualified it by saying he had acquaintances rather than friends, who were people he had met through care. Another said he had cousins who were involved, and two said they had brothers who were or had been involved in car crime at some time.

All of the young people interviewed took cars with others. They gave the impression that they viewed it as a social activity. Most of them would go out with the same friends each night. The numbers in the group would vary from two to about 20.

Within most groups there would be a great deal of co-operation and team work. Certain members would carry out the tasks they did best.

> *"Sometimes we have our own job to do when we're getting into a car. I'm better at getting in through the doors, so once I've done the door, I just let the others carry on and once they've started it, then I drive".*

> *"Each of us would have a job to do. We'd pinch a couple of cars and then whoever got to the car first would be the one who broke into it."*

One of those interviewed referred to the group he went around with as having a 'Manager' and 'Assistant Manager.'

> *"I'm the Assistant Manager. The Manager's the best at stealing cars - he can do a car quickest. But when he's inside [a young offender institute] I'm the Manager. He's the best driver as well. Nigel Mansell, that's what we call him. He's been driving since he was really young. He went to ....[a young offender institute] and he learnt loads of things there."*

It became obvious talking to the young people that they knew boys by reputation from other districts. Many of them had met in care institutions.

"I met a lot of them in ...[care institution] Other people who were in there with me — their friends would come up to see them and that's how we all got to know each other. Or they'd take me up to their area and I'd get to meet more of their friends. We all know everyone else who takes cars in this area and other areas."

"We would know who was good at doing it and we'd know what type of car they'd taken."

Eleven of those interviewed said they had at some time shown someone else how to get into cars and start them.

"The purpose was to get more people involved. They saw me doing it and they'd want to know what to do."

The following quote illustrates their code of ethics:

"I wouldn't teach anyone to get them into trouble but if they're already in trouble and they came along, they could watch."

Eleven of the 17 interviewed said they had took cars on their own but they would only do so for a purpose. The most common reason was needing to get somewhere after absconding from care.

Two of those interviewed said they would do both.

"When I'm on my own, I only get a few cars a day. When I go with my friends, we time ourselves pinching the cars. When I'm with friends we take a lot of cars and we see who can do them the quickest and things like that."

"Both, depending on my mood and the reason, because the reason changed with the mood. I think the majority of times it would be with other people but I have taken cars on my own just for the sake of taking one. It was the same people on some occasions but the people would vary a lot of the time."

3. THE PROCESS OF TAKING A CAR

The young people interviewed answered a series of questions which outlined the process of taking a car from the initial thought to what they did with the car once they had taken it.

21

Decision to take a car

They were asked to identify what would make them decide to take a car at any one time. With some, the impulse would be spontaneous.

> *"We'd just want to if we saw one."*

Half responded by saying they would do it for fun because they were bored and one said he did it because others influenced him. Another felt that there was more to it and referred to taking a car as an addiction. Two gave specific reasons such as wanting to abscond from care or use the car to commit a burglary. One young person said he gained self-esteem from taking cars:

> *"A reason would be to say I can do it. I could take a car. The buzz when you are in a stolen car and you've got the police chasing you gives you such a rush of adrenalin that you know you want to do it again. And then you might be out with a few friends and decide to take them. I think the other reason is to me to say look I can take a car. Look at me I can do this."*

Those interviewed were asked if they ever planned to take a car. Eight said they always planned it; five said they never planned it, they would just be out and take one; and four said they would do both.

> *"Both. Sometimes I'd just go out to shop lift and when I'm in a shop I'd pinch a screwdriver, then I'd go and take a car. Mostly, I'd go out planning to take them. Sometimes I'd pinch six or seven in a day but it gets boring after a while. "*

One young person looked on it as more of a challenge:

> *"We'd be out when we'd take cars. For example we'd go to Ponty(pridd) with a train ticket and then we'd throw our train tickets away so we'd have to get it, take a car in order to get home."*

Means of entry

The methods of getting into a car and starting it were common to all those interviewed, although it depended on the type of car. The comments have been edited to avoid graphic descriptions of how to break into a car.

"I can think of four different ways off the top of my head. It depends basically on the type of car. The most common I've taken are Fords and Vauxhalls really. The reason being that they're so easy to access and to drive..."

All of the 17 interviewed identified using a screwdriver as the most popular means of entry, mainly for Vauxhall cars. Other means were using keys or smashing a window.

Once inside the car, the group would begin working as a team, which would include making sure they didn't get caught.

"There will always be someone standing by (in another car) so we can get away. We normally have about two in a car trying to get it started and we normally have someone looking out to see if anyone is coming. We normally have two cars going at one time. I like getting into cars and I'm probably the fastest so I normally do that, but my mate's a better driver so I normally then — once I've started it — let him get in the driving seat."

All those interviewed said they would lock themselves in the car while they were trying to start it to protect themselves from the owner should s/he return.

Ways of starting a car

Three ways of starting a car were identified. These were:

> keys
> 'black boxing'
> 'hot wiring'.

The most common method seemed to be 'black boxing', with all respondents mentioning this as a way they had started cars. The term refers to the box behind the ignition barrel. 'Hot wiring' was not a method favoured by many, as it appeared to be far more complicated than black boxing.

Many talked about the problem of snapping the steering lock, which needed a great deal of strength. The time it takes to get into a car and start it varies depending on the skill of those involved. Times ranged from seven seconds to 40 seconds. Many said they would time each other to see who could do it fastest.

After the car had been started, the next step, the young people said, would be to check how much fuel was in the tank:

"You first look at the petrol gauge and if it's low you then pull into a garage and get some petrol. You get some and just drive off. It's not any more of a risk as the police are probably looking for you anyway."

4. TYPES OF CARS

All the interviewees were asked which types of cars they normally looked for. Their answers corresponded to the data from the police juvenile records showing which cars were commonly taken (Figure 3, page 14). The cars at highest risk were Vauxhalls, both Astras and Cavaliers, due to their easy access and performance.

Many respondents said that initially they would usually take any type of car and would then look for a better one, always having the first car ready to jump into and get away if anyone should disturb them.]

"Normally we would take one car that we know is easier to take and then we will drive off and try to get another one. If we can't start it then we'd just jump back into the other one and drive away. Sometimes we will try out different cars that we've never taken before but only if we've got one standing by that we can get away in."

All respondents said they would go for fast cars, ones with fuel injection engines only, as any other car would be too slow.

"You need a car with a big engine in it: twin fuel injection turbo. It's not worth pinching an 1100 because if you got chased by the law, then they'd just catch you right away. You've got to have something to be able to drop them."

When the young people were asked which makes of cars they would not take, Ladas and Skodas were the most common answers given by nearly everyone. Otherwise, they would take any type of car if they needed it to get somewhere. But if they were going to race the car, they would be looking for a new (no older than 'C' registration), fast model.

"The easiest to take is a Vauxhall, or the really old Fords like Capris or Cortinas. They're really easy, but the newest models of Fords are quite hard. Vauxhalls are really easy — they think

24

> *they've got it dead-locked but you can still get into them in about ten seconds. I reckon the hardest I've ever tried is a Saab. I wouldn't take any car, not really. I wouldn't take a shed — a crap car. If it's over C reg then I'll pinch it, whatever type of car it is."*

Although all were clear about the easiest cars to take, one had difficulty identifying a car that was difficult to take. Others mentioned names, but there was no consensus. It would seem that once a young person has learnt how to get into a certain type of car, it then becomes easy. The problem seemed to be learning how to get into new cars — having the time to do it, while trying not to get caught. Cars which some identified as being easy were said by others to be difficult, which illustrates that getting into certain makes of car is an acquired skill and no car is exempt. Some cars were perhaps easy to get into but difficult to start.

Unless the cars were taken because the person wanted to get some-where or use it for another crime, then more than one car would be taken in any evening.

> *"We'd take about ten cars in a night to show off. We'd take one and then we'd see a better one and then we'd take that one. We just keep going until we get a better, faster car each time. We'd have two cars sometimes with some of us in each one. One gang in one and another gang in another. We'd follow each other around in the cars."*

> *"We normally take more than one car, we would take as many as we could in one night and sometimes we'd have a number of cars at the same time and we'd all drive them together. Other times we'd take one car then take another one and dump the first one and then take another one and dump the second one. Some of us are better at driving than others so we would do most of the driving."*

All the young people were asked what was their favourite car. Some had difficulty in identifying one as, they said, there were so many. Others talked about the ones they liked stealing most, and others talked about the car they would like to own. Porsche was a popular answer.

5. TIME OF DAY

There was no consensus about whether it was easier to take cars during the day or night. Instead, it was often a matter of preference. Some believed there was more chance of being chased by the police at night while others believed the opposite. The data from the police juvenile records seem largely to bear this out, as although there were peaks and troughs over the 24-hour period, cars were stolen during both the day and night.

One respondent said he took cars only during the day. Eight said they took them during the night, and eight said they would take them at any time. Of these eight, two said they would prefer to take them during the night and one preferred during the day, but the rest (five) had no preference. This is what one person had to say about it:

> *"It depends. If I really wanted to go somewhere desperate, then I'd take a car whatever time of day it was, but if I didn't, then I'd just wait for one. I'd just wait for the night and until the other boys could come out with me. It's harder during the day, you've got more chance of being chased and being seen. As soon as they see your face, then they start chasing you. If we take a car in the night, then we can keep it all night, we don't have to keep changing it."*

6. LOCATIONS FROM WHICH CARS ARE TAKEN

The locations from where young people said they took cars varied. Car parks were most common for taking cars during the day.

> *"We take them from car parks. You know you've got at least ten minutes to take it, even if they've only gone in for one thing. We would watch them leave their cars. In the evenings we'd take them off the street, then wherever they are we'd just pinch them."*

For some, the location of a car did not matter:

> *"If there's a car there, and you want it, you take it."*

During the evening, cars are mainly taken from the roadside, or from people's drives. Some of the interviewees believed it was easier to take cars from driveways as there was more chance of finding them unlocked and it was usually relatively dark. Two of those interviewed said they took cars only from car showrooms.

Cars were taken from many towns, but the most common areas from which the young people said they took cars were Pontypridd and Bridgend. This was irrespective of where the young people lived. It is interesting to note that these two towns both have institutions where young people are placed in care. Two of those asked said they would not take a car from near where they lived because they believed they should not 'do it to their own kind'.

Nearly half the respondents (eight) said they would take more than one car in a night from different areas.

> *"I'd take them from anywhere really. If I was in Ponty(pridd), I would take one from there, and then drive to another place, and then take one from there."*

7. DRIVING

All but one young person had driven a car. They said that some were not such good drivers and although everyone would have a go, it would mainly be in car parks, not on the road in case they were chased by the police.

> *"Some of them drive, but not all the time in case we were chased by the police. They would let them have a go if we were in the car park or something, but not when we were on the roads, 'cos they would not be able to handle it if they were chased by the police and had to go a lot faster."*

All the young people were asked to rate themselves as drivers. The responses ranged from 'don't know' to 'not bad for my age' and 'pretty good'. The majority felt they were adequate. The following quote shows how one young person assessed himself:

> *"Most of my friends are better than me but I'm better than someone's who's passed their test — which isn't that good in the car thief world."*

Another young person explained how he viewed his driving skills:

> *"I don't really know how I rate myself as a driver. I don't see myself as the next Nigel Mansell. Adequate, I can drive as well*

> *as the next man. The thing that gives you the edge over the police is the fact that you don't care and you will drive places that the police won't because it's not your car. You basically don't think as much about yourself, in a sense that you take a risk that the police wouldn't. So in the majority of times you have got something that they haven't. You've got an edge on them and you are driving in such a way that you are bound to get away from them, but I wouldn't rate myself as a particularly great driver."*

Another answered with equal honesty saying he didn't rate himself particularly highly:

> *"Sick, when I'm on the road I've got no sense. I just put my foot down on the floor. The group I go with, none of the others really drive it's just me that drives. The others can drive but I'd be the better driver if we were chased by the police. The others mainly drive when we are on waste ground."*

Fastest speed
All the interviewees were asked the fastest speed they had ever done, and why. Two said they had done 145 mph and all but one said they had driven over 100 mph.

Nine had done their fastest speed while being chased by the police. Six said they were just trying the car out to see how fast it would go, and the rest (two) were racing with others in another stolen car.

Highway Code
When asked if they had read the Highway Code, five young people said yes, twelve said no. Of those twelve, six said they knew most of the road signs.

Alcohol and drugs
Of those interviewed, three admitted to having been drunk while taking cars and four to having taken drugs. Some said they would never drink and drive.

> *" If I was going to take a car, I'd rather be sober than drunk."*

Some believed they were more likely to get caught if they were drunk.

"I think I was only drunk once, but it deadens the adrenaline buzz, so its no good really and that was the time when I actually got done for taking a car."

8. CAR CHASES

All of those interviewed said they had been involved in a police chase at some time. Some saw this as part of the thrill.

"A lot of the time it gives you such a buzz that you hope that you are going to get chased by them."

"The thrill you get out of being chased by the police is amazing."

One person said that occasionally he would incite a police chase.

"Sometimes we stop the car and flash them so that they can catch up with us."

Most would remain calm if they saw a police car until they were sure that it was going to chase them.

"We used to ignore them mostly if we saw them when we were driving along. We'd just carry on until we were sure they were going to chase us and then we'd put our foot down."

The majority felt that the police would only chase them during the evening, as it was too dangerous during the day.

"We'd be chased mostly during the night, very rarely during the day."

Others said they were chased during the day and night. A small number felt they were better drivers than the police because they were never caught during chases.

"I don't think the police are very good drivers. They just don't take as many risks as we do. We're always taking the risks and driving too fast. Well I've lost a couple of Jaguars and they're very powerful cars and I've lost them in a Cavalier."

29

Others appreciated the reasons why the police may call off a chase:

"You know they are not going to chase you through a built-up area because you might kill someone, so they stop."

"The police have to call off the chases most of the time because we were driving too recklessly."

The police are the first to acknowledge the risks of putting an inexperienced driver under pressure in a powerful car and have sometimes had to abandon pursuit where it was feared there would be an accident. This decision is not made by the police officer in pursuit but by another officer in a control room who has a better overview of the situation. It is unfortunate that this decision is viewed by the young people as a 'victory' and reinforces their own perceptions of their driving skills.

Some of those interviewed did try to avoid being chased by the police.

"We normally sit it out but then if he starts putting his lights on and coming up behind, then we will put our foot down. We normally go towards the lanes if we are being chased because that's the only way we can get away from them, because the police cars go fast. They've got fast cars now."

"If I was out and I saw a police car, then I'd slow down and use the indicators and everything and pretend everything was OK. I'd just behave as if it was my own car, and sometimes we'd try and wipe all our prints off and run like mad if we were being chased."

All of them said they would only drive on roads they knew, so that if they were chased by the police, they would know which roads to go down to get away.

Racing cars
All those interviewed said they had raced cars at some time. It was viewed as a popular pastime. Sometimes this would be planned, and a group of young people would go out and take more than one car so they could race. At other times, one group might meet another group in a car and they would begin to race. Where and when they would race cars would vary: day or night, waste ground or main roads.

"Sometimes, we go and race against each other. If someone else had taken a car, there would be about ten to twenty people involved and we'd all take turns."

"We were being chased by some other kids in another car. We'd all gone out together, and we'd taken two cars, and we were racing them. We do that often."

9. THEFT FROM CARS

All of those interviewed admitted taking articles from a car they had stolen. The most common items to be taken were stereos, tapes, speakers, money and clothing.

Only a few (four) said that they would occasionally take a car for its contents but normally they would take the car for itself and then see what was in it. As one young person expressed it:

"We'd be silly not to take anything from it."

The young people were also asked whether they had damaged cars after they had finished with them. Three said they had burnt them out occasionally but not every time. Some (five) believed it to be a way of ensuring they would not get caught. Others (four) said there was no need to burn a car out as the police did not take fingerprints unless the car had been involved in a chase.

Four said they had damaged cars while driving them or had deliberately damaged them because they had been stolen for the insurance money. The rest (13) said they would not damage cars. One person said he had initially but then stopped:

" Mindless vandalism, yes, I think only on two or three occasions when we just damaged the car for no reason. We just smashed up everything we could. But towards the latter stages we'd be more   constructive in a sense and start stripping it and taking the parts. The reason some people damage cars is so that there is no evidence left, so that they can't find fingerprints."

10. MOTIVATION

All those interviewed were asked to explain in their own words the reasons why they took cars. Most of them gave more than one reason (table 2).

Although the most popular response was 'for money', the impression gained was that this was an added opportunistic advantage of taking cars and not always the main motivation. The reasons why the young people took cars are best explained in their own words.

> *"People get kicks out of it. People like having chases off the police. They like seeing who's the best driver. They like to see how fast they can go in cars, and generally have a good time. It's everything to do with cars, not just one thing. Different people get different things out of it. Like I don't nick cars for the kicks all the time, sometimes I do, but other times I nick the cars to get out of the area."*

> *"I don't know really but you get a good feeling when you are in a car. It's just you."*

Table 2

Reasons why cars were taken	Number giving that reason
For money (selling parts, insurance job)	11
Fun, buzz, good feeling	9
To drive	5
Boredom	4
To get somewhere (especially if absconded)	4
For the chase (by Police)	3
Showing off	2
To do a job	2
Challenge	1
Can get away with it	1
Helping friends out	1
To do something I can do well	1
To do something illegal	1
To see who's the best	1

"Most people take cars because there's nothing else to do, there's nothing at all to do anywhere up here. Most people pinch cars out of boredom."

One of the older people interviewed had the following to say about why young people took cars:

"There are a number of reasons. One is the thrill of the chase. The thrill of doing something you are not supposed to. Can I take the car when it's not mine, and if I take it what can I do with it? I suppose all in all it's just adolescence mainly because you are not supposed to do it. There are lots of reasons really but I think there is one key reason which is at the centre of a lot of reasons — which is the reason why everything gets taken. It's just the level of understanding that you are at, at that point of time. We all have different reasons at different times. There comes a point when they say knowledge is dangerous and you just do things that you know a little bit about, but you know that you really shouldn't do them. You have no respect for the law and that's one way of showing it. You only start respecting the laws of society if you are a law-abiding citizen and the stage I was at, I was not considering myself as such. You are not above the law as such, but you just don't respect it. Young people, they just don't understand it."

Taking cars for profit

The same young person explained why, in his experience, cars were taken for money:

"Only at the later stages [did I think about money]. *First of all it was all joyriding different cars, trying it out but towards the end of my actual period I started thinking, well OK, what else can I get out of it? I get a buzz and I get a thrill, and all that, and more street credibility, but what else can I get out of it? And I thought, what if I start selling these cars, because some of the cars I was driving were £10,000 to £12,000, so I really could get something out of it. So yes, towards the end — which I'd say came with experience — I would try and get something else out of it other than just a buzz."*

When asked further about taking cars for money, most of the young people said that at some stage they had been asked by others either to get parts for cars or 'to do an insurance job' for someone, i.e. the owner asked them to burn out his/her car so that he/she could make an insurance claim.

> *"Yes, I have been asked. It probably happens quite often. They're mainly people who are much older than me who own their own cars, and they want spare parts. I've been asked to do an insurance job too. That happens quite often."*

The rate for an 'insurance job' seemed to be between £100 and £200.

There was a suggestion from some of organized crime, with groups of local adults asking the young people to get them parts. When the young people were questioned more about this during the interviews, they became reticent, but the majority of them admitted it did happen.

With some young people, the initiative to make money was obviously their own.

> *"I once stole a car which was about £17,000 in the showroom, and I sold it for about £400. Whoever bought that got a good deal."*

Others said they would incorporate making money with having fun too.

> *"We'd take a car for someone to sell. We'd take it up and drop it off, get all the stuff off, give it to them, have our money and then we'd pinch another car and come back down, and just drive around in it for the rest of the night. There's no point in pinching a car and not driving around in it."*

The young people interviewed were all asked to state what they most enjoyed about taking cars (table 3).

It is interesting to note that the reason 'to drive' was rated as highly as 'excitement'. Taking cars for money was almost last on the list, which confirms that making money is opportunism rather than the main motivation.

From talking to these young people, some of them gave the impression that they were addicted to taking cars. The addiction appeared to be the excitement.

> *"I think the adrenalin is the addiction, not actually stealing the car but it's the buzz that is addictive..."*

Table 3

Most enjoyed about taking cars	Number giving that reason
Buzz, makes you happy, excitement	5
To drive	5
Don't know	3
Money	2
To race	1

Reasons for stopping

The young people were asked what would make them stop taking cars, or if they had stopped, what was it that had made them. Four young people said they hoped they had stopped taking cars.

> *"Yes, there are a few reasons why I stopped. I'd had a custodial sentence for eight months for three 'take and drive aways' [TDAs] and prior to those three I hadn't taken a car for eight to ten months, which is quite a long time. Now the reason I stopped then was because I just didn't feel like doing it any more. I'd got all the buzz I needed out of it. But eight months later, a friend came to me and said he needed a car. He wanted a couple of wheels from a car and asked me whether I could find them for him, but prior to that I stopped because I wanted to stop. It doesn't matter what anyone says to you, you've got to want to do it and you won't stop until you're ready and no amount of help will matter until you're ready for the help."*

> *"I was getting too much hassle with people, hassle from the owners' of the cars — they'd come round to my house and say you've taken my car. I was also getting hassle from the police — if anyone ever reported a car stolen they would immediately come around to my house to see where I was."*

One person who, in his own words, had classed taking cars as 'an addiction' said he had stopped for the following reasons:

> *"Because I'm getting on a bit now, and I'm looking for work. But I'd still do insurance jobs now. If someone came up to me and paid me £50 to take their car with a key, then I would do it.*

> *It's money in my pocket. You are not ripping off the owners then, you're just ripping off the insurance companies and they've got millions and millions of pounds anyway."*

Three interviewees felt that once they had cars of their own, they would not take other cars anymore.

> *" I wouldn't pinch them then. I'd just get done for driving with no insurance. I wouldn't get done for TDA."*

For one interviewee, even having a car of his own would not stop him.

> *"If I had a car of my own, I would nick a car then, to get parts off it."*

One of the older people interviewed was asked whether he felt it was something most young people would grow out of:

> *"Now that depends on the reasons you are doing it for. I think it depends on the reason first why you might stop. I did a lot of it for the respect of my own peers and also because it was the buzz, especially when you are being chased by the police. But some people don't grow out of it because they are in it for different reasons. If they have other reasons than the thrill or the buzz, then they will not stop taking them ever."*

The reasons for stopping (given by those who hoped they had actually stopped) and the reasons that other interviewees suggested might make them stop in the future are summarized in table 4:

Table 4

Reasons for stopping	Number giving that reason
Accidents	2
Don't want to do it anymore	2
Getting into too much trouble both with Police and owners of cars	2
Had a custodial sentence	1
Friend in prison	1
Trying to get work	1
Met another boy in YOI convicted of manslaughter after knocking someone over	1

Six of those interviewed said that they had not stopped. Although they felt they would have to stop sometime, they said they did not know how to. One young man was adamant about not stopping.

"No, I haven't stopped. Nothing would make me."

None of those who said they had not stopped could think of anything that might help them to do so.

"I usually go when I'm in a bad temper, see. I like driving."

Motor Projects

Some felt that having access to a motor project would not make them stop, as the excitement was in doing something illegal.

"I think the adrenaline is the addiction, not actually stealing the car but it's the buzz that is addictive and in all the schemes in the world, you won't get that sort of buzz. You can drive as many cars as you like on a racetrack and you won't get the same buzz as doing something wrong basically. So that's why schemes wouldn't work for me but for some people they might if they're stealing them for different reasons."

Two felt that being part of a motor project may have had some impact on them:

"I think it [the motor project] *may have slowed me down, definitely slowed me down, but not stopped me altogether. I was taking them mainly for the excitement. There'd be no fun if you weren't nicking them."*

"Yes, if I knew I could do that [take part in motor project] *and I know that if I got caught pinching another car, I wouldn't be able to go to it again, then yes, I might stop."*

11. DETERRENTS

All the young people were questioned about devices fitted to cars as theft deterrents.

Alarms
All of those interviewed had taken cars equipped with alarms. Some had learnt techniques which made it easy for them to get past certain makes of alarms, while others found the same makes of alarm difficult. It is therefore not possible to come to any conclusions as to which type of alarm provides the strongest deterrent.

In general, it appeared that alarms did act as a minor deterrent, since taking a car with an alarm meant spending a longer time in disabling it.

> *"Alarms would present a difficulty, but you just think this is going to be more hard, so it's going to take more time. But if you want it then it doesn't make any difference at all, it's just another three or four minutes on the time."*

> *"Alarms wouldn't really stop people, but say there were two cars parked together, and one had an alarm, and one didn't, then you're bound to pick the one without the alarm ... it's quite easy to stop alarms if you know how to do them, but there's not many people who do, well not many people I know that can do it."*

One respondent said a car alarm had deterred him.

> *"They do work, most of them. I know people who can get into cars with alarms. I can't because I haven't got the knowledge."*

Although only one respondent admitted that a car alarm had deterred him, when the young people were asked how they would prevent a car of their own being taken, 11 said they would install a car alarm. Some would not specify the make of alarm other than it must be a 'tidy one'. Others did give brand names but, again, there was no consensus as to which were the better ones.

One person felt that alarms were no deterrent at all:

> *"Burglar alarms don't deter people. If someone wants your car then they'll take it. If you want a car badly then you take it no matter what."*

38

Other physical devices
Other responses to the question of how the young people would prevent a car of their own being stolen were: electrify the door handle; put the car in a garage; take a part out of the engine; sleep in the car; keep a Rottweiler in the back seat; fit a steering lock that will not snap; and fit a Stoplock.

Everyone was asked if there was anything that had ever deterred them from taking a car. Nine said nothing had ever deterred them. Three said that they had been deterred by other people, either the owner of the car or passers-by who felt something was suspicious. The remaining five mentioned the following physical devices:

> Wheel clamps
> Autolocks and crook locks (at first)
> Stoplock

(A Stoplock is a steering wheel immobiliser which prevents the steering wheel from being turned because of its long arm.)

> *"Wheel clamps, the auto locks that go from the hand brake to the gear stick are a waste of time and umbrellas going from the steering wheel to the pedals, they're a waste of time as well. There's one lock that stops you though which has a yellow arm which will go through the windscreen if you try to turn the steering wheel."*

The Police
All those interviewed were asked whether they considered the police as a deterrent. From their responses, it appeared that most of them would try not to think about anything that might worry them:

> *"I never thought about them. I just blanked it off when I got in the car."*

> *"At the time I wasn't worried about them. I didn't think about the police. I didn't think about my parents or knocking anyone over. I didn't think about anything like that."*

Some interviewees thought about the police occasionally:

> *"I would worry about them only when I saw them if I was driving. Other than that, I didn't think about them that much. I used to think they were just doing their job really."*

> *"It didn't stop me. People who take cars don't really think about the consequences, they just take them. You don't often think about the police when you're taking a car. If you want a car then you just take it. It doesn't matter whether the police are going to chase you or not."*

Vehicle Watch

The young people were also questioned about the Vehicle Watch Scheme. Car owners who are members of the Scheme display a sticker on their windscreen. Cars displaying these stickers are more likely to be stopped by the police between the hours of midnight and 5 a.m. The Scheme was introduced by South Wales Police in 1990.

Only two of the young people had never seen a sticker; the rest had seen them, but did not think they acted as a deterrent for a number of different reasons:

> *(1) "You can peel them off. I know you are not supposed to be able to but you can."*

> *(2) "They don't really matter because if the police are going to pull you over, then they will anyway, whether you've got a sticker in or not."*

> *(3) "Where I live I've never seen the police around."*

> *(4) "All that's to do with is in the early hours of the morning, but we mostly pinch them in the day, so it wouldn't apply to us."*

One young person suggested that a sticker may be an added advantage:

> *"Some joyriders like to have the police chasing. A Vehicle Watch sticker may make them take a car because they'll know then that the police may be chasing them later."*

12. CONSEQUENCES

All those interviewed were asked whether they considered the consequences of what they were doing. For example, having an accident, getting caught, or being disqualified from driving. They were also asked whether they thought about the owner of the car.

Accidents

Six said they had never thought about having an accident; the others said they thought about it but it did not stop them.

> *"Only if I was going fast on the motorway and then I would sometimes think about it."*

These responses do, however, contradict to some extent the reasons young people gave for having stopped taking cars, when two said that they had stopped because of accidents (table 4, page 36).

One person who had had a serious accident said that he did think about it more now:

> *"If I'm driving now and I go above a certain speed, I start shaking and I sometimes freeze in the car. I just sit there and stare."*

Although almost half said they never thought about having an accident, 15 of the 17 interviewed said they had been involved in an accident at some stage. Two of these had been involved in very serious ones. The rest described accidents which sounded serious but they had managed to escape with few injuries. Most of them said they considered themselves lucky. Six said the accident had happened while they were being chased by the police.

One young man, when asked whether an accident had ever put him off, said:

> *"No. You've got to die some day, so you may as well die young. It's better than living 'til you're older."*

The two young men who had been involved in serious accidents were asked whether they had been in a car since. They replied:

> *"Yes, the day I came out of hospital, but I probably drive very carefully now. I haven't pinched a car now for six weeks, I'm trying to stop it. It's a long time for me, because I'm normally out every day pinching them."*

> *"Yes, only once, but I've stopped it since then. As soon as I got off my crutches, I just saw a group of friends who were pinching cars, and thought I'd go with them, but we got caught, so I haven't bothered since then."*

41

Getting caught

Half said they never thought about getting caught; the other half said they did but it would not stop them taking cars, they would just be more careful. One person did say the thought of getting caught had an effect on his actions:

> *"Yes, that's one of the things which made me stop. I used to get panicky sometimes if I saw the police. Most times that would happen I'd just leave the car and get out and run."*

Disqualification from driving

None of those interviewed ever thought about being disqualified from driving. Most had already been disqualified anyway.

> *"Not one bit no, because most of the time I didn't have a licence. I was banned for two years altogether. It took me a long time to get a licence but most of the time it didn't enter your head at all. I think a lot of that was to do with my age because I didn't think about licences at all when I was younger. People who are in the state of mind to steal a car don't really think about licences at all because it's not relevant because they are not going to have one for a long time."*

Ownership

The young people were asked a series of questions about ownership to determine their views on the nature of their offence. Some believed that they only took the cars of people who could afford it; others said they did very little damage to the car so the owner would get it back eventually and it would still be in a good condition. All of them, however, expected the owner to 'beat them up' if they were discovered by them. Here is what one young person had to say about ownership:

> *"If someone stole my car, I think I would be extremely upset and I'd probably go after them. But at the end of the day, a car is a car and if I can take it and you can't keep it then that's your problem and I'm going to take it. It's not my fault that you can't keep it, but that's not necessarily right but that's the way people think. The car's there so I can take it. If I can take it then I will and I won't think about the owner."*

42

This person was asked if he thought it was the owner's fault for not making the car properly secure:

"In some respects, but obviously no. No, it's not the owner's fault. Why should he have to make it really secure? That's just the society we live in, it's real. If you can't keep it and I can take it then it's mine, but then when the police take it back it isn't mine any more because I can't keep it anymore and as long as I can keep it then I will. Yes, so in some ways it's the owner's fault."

Five of those interviewed said they never thought about the owner of the car at all. Five said they would never take the car of someone they knew:

"I wouldn't take the car of someone I knew because you don't do it to your own kind. You do it to other people who've got the money. The cars we take are new cars so the people must have a lot of money."

Two said they worried in case the owner was big:

"I'd think if he was a big man like then I was going to get a kicking off him but we'd normally lock ourselves in the car. We'd lock the doors straight away. Quite a few times we've been stuck in the car and the bloke's been kicking and punching the window and then we'd try and start it quick and just drive off."

The rest said they thought about the owner sometimes:

"I sometimes wait to see someone coming out of the car. If I saw an old bloke coming out of a car, I wouldn't touch it but if I saw a 'yuppyish' person then I wouldn't mind because yuppies are like posh and all that and there's not much damage, like an Astra, no damage at all really from stealing it."

All the young people were asked what they would think about someone who stole a car that they owned. Seven of the young people said it was a difficult question for them to answer. Four said they wouldn't mind.

"I wouldn't think badly about them, as I do it myself. If I had it insured it wouldn't bother me so much because I'd get the insurance. If I wasn't insured and they took it then I'd kill them."

Six respondents spoke equally strongly, saying they would 'beat them up' and that this was also what they expected from the owners of the cars they took. One young person explained that it was the car that mattered and the owner was often ignored in the process:

> *"Ninety-nine per cent of the time, I never really analysed what I was doing and I never really thought about who owned the car and I never really thought that if I took the car then that car would not be the same to the owner after they had got it back. But most of the time you just think it's a car that you want so I wouldn't regard the owner at all. You don't really think it's the end of the world to take someone's car."*

The professionals' view

Six social workers were interviewed and questionnaires were completed by five police officers. All respondents viewed car crime involving young people to be a major problem in their area. Social workers perceived car crime as a group activity, with most young people introduced to it by older, more experienced thieves. It was seen by them as something most young people grew out of:

> "It's part of growing up, a phase they go through. Then something more attractive comes along: girls, their own bedsit, a full-time job as opposed to Youth Training and then they go along another channel."

One social worker stressed the fact that the young people needed a positive replacement for taking cars and used as an example the case of one young person who was a prolific car offender. When he was in the care of the local authority, he gained status within his peer group from taking cars and he felt he had nothing to lose. After a custodial sentence, a placement was found for him with a family and he stopped taking cars for four months. He started again when he was having problems at school and his family placement began to go wrong. He said that if there was something else in his life, he did not need cars.

The social workers believed that a young person's main motivation for taking cars was for the 'buzz' and excitement, which they saw as an 'addiction'. They felt that little was currently being done in their area to tackle the problem. Most were of the opinion that prevention was better than searching for a 'cure'. They proposed that activities provided for young people needed to acknowledge their interest in cars and driving so that attempts could be made to channel this interest constructively. Suggestions included providing young people with access to a motor project and/or driving lessons at school.

The majority of the social workers interviewed also felt that the recession contributed greatly to the problem of juvenile car crime. They believed that poor housing, lack of education and job opportunities, and the low level of Income Support all gave young people little hope of anything to work for. They also felt that car security needed to be improved.

Police officers saw car crime among young people as an increasing problem in their areas. They believed it to be a group activity, mainly within the 14- to 20-year-old age group. They felt that the main motivations of the young people involved were to maintain their peer group image and to portray an anti-authoritarian attitude. The need for more crime prevention was stressed.

Many believed that children should be educated at school about the dangers of taking cars and a number advocated the use of a secure unit in Wales for offenders. They also felt that harsher sentences should be imposed by the courts. In addition, many recommended that car security should be improved by manufacturers.

PART III

WHAT CAN BE DONE?

Responses to car crime

A number of initiatives have been developed in recent years in response to the growth of car crime. Our consideration of proposals for a way forward in terms of reducing the incidence of car crime in Mid Glamorgan was informed by a review of some of these initiatives.

Deterrent sentences for offenders

The Aggravated Vehicle-Taking Act of 1992 represents a move to 'toughen up' on the offenders, curbing car crime through the use of deterrent sentences: the Act increases the courts' powers for imposing custodial sentences on car thieves (and see page 10).

When introducing the Aggravated Vehicle-Taking Bill in 1991, Kenneth Baker MP, then Home Secretary, suggested that such a move was necessary:

> "to stop the plague of car crime getting out of hand".

Roy Hattersley MP, then Shadow Home Secretary, disagreed. He predicted that the measures contained within the Bill would have little or no impact on the teenagers inolved in most car crime. In his view, the group which the Bill sought to target were:

> "uniquely unlikely to be deterred by the threat of even the most extreme penalties. Deterrence only has an effect on the rational

47

> *men and women who calculate the consequences of their actions".*

The interviews with social workers and police for this study took place shortly after the Act was introduced. Both were asked for their views on the new legislation. Social workers generally saw it as a response to genuine fears and anger expressed by communities, but questioned its validity as a deterrent. They felt that young people who commit crimes do not think of the consequences and that the imposition of tougher penalties would not therefore deter them from offending. They questioned custodial sentences generally, seeing them as a way of enabling young offenders to pass on ideas and techniques about crimes.

The police welcomed the legislation as a step in the right direction but were more cautious about its long-term effects, preferring to wait before deciding whether it had any impact as a deterrent.

Reviews of statistics and of other research, carried out for the purposes of this study, suggest that increased use of custodial sentences has little impact as a deterrent. Nationally, more than 70% of young offenders released from custody re-offend within two years. A recent study in a neighbouring authority to Mid Glamorgan showed that between 1989 and 1991, all juveniles who received a custodial sentence for offences involving vehicles re-offended on release. Many did so on the same date they were released, most within three months and all within 12 months (Isles, 1992).

The Home Office's own working party on car crime (1988) concluded that:

> *"a custodial sentence may not only fail in many cases to prevent further offending but can indeed provide status and education in crime".*

Alternative responses

It was the overwhelming failure of custodial sentences to stem the rise in car crime that led to the setting up of the multi-agency initiative in South Wales (South Wales Juvenile and Young Persons Auto-Crime Standing Committee) and subsequently this research. All the agencies involved were becoming increasingly frustrated and concerned that no existing response was curtailing the offending behaviour of persistent, young, car thieves.

In our endeavour to identify success in combating car crime, we reviewed categories of responses not specifically based on a deterrent value, most notably those:

i) which aim to provide comparable interest and excitement to known offenders in a safe and legal environment. Such projects, known loosely as 'motor projects' have demonstrated some success in reducing re-offending amongst convicted young offenders.

ii) with a focus on prevention, with measures aimed at reducing the opportunity for car crime.

Both these types of responses to car crime bore relationship to a number of key themes that had emerged from our schedule of interviews with young offenders: the desire for excitement; the lack of self-esteem; the influence of peer pressure; and the apparent opportunism characterizing juvenile car crime. The study sought to review the effectiveness of these responses and to gain the views of police and social workers as to their value. The role of the media's glamorization of cars was also briefly examined.

Motor projects: providing a legal opportunity for young people to drive

Motor projects have come to be regarded by many working with juvenile offenders as being an acceptable and successful means of diverting young people away from vehicle-related crime.

The term motor project is used to describe a wide variety of activities involving young people with cars, go-carts or motor cycles. Projects may be for the use of a whole community or set up specifically as alternatives to custody for known offenders. Their activities can range from racing cars round on a track for a few hours a week, to schemes that also work on offending behaviour and offer young people the opportunity to build on their social skills.

As part of The Children's Society's research into possible responses to car crime in Mid Glamorgan, a wide range of data on motor projects was collated: information on existing motor projects was obtained from the National Association of Motor Projects (NAMP); a literature review was conducted in an attempt to obtain evaluative material; initiatives currently operating in South Wales were examined; professionals (police and social workers) were asked for their views on motor projects. The findings are presented below.

Do motor projects work? — the evidence

In 1992, Thames Valley Police carried out a survey of existing motor projects, prior to setting up a multi–agency motor scheme. Although none of the project workers were prepared to give examples of their own statistics, they quoted figures produced by NAMP:

What can be done?

Eight out of ten sent to prison for car crime, re-offended within two years. Seven out of ten who stay with a motor project for over three months do not re-offend within two years.

Oxfordshire conducted a telephone survey of local police where motor projects were in operation and found considerable support for the schemes. They concluded that early indicators are that motor projects have been successful in many areas of the country.

In 1988, the Home Office Working Group on car crime carried out a survey of the 25 projects which had formed themselves into NAMP. They found that the majority of the projects were funded and managed by either the Probation Service, Youth Service or Social Services; the rest were organized by the voluntary sector. Four of the projects were for non-offenders; the rest provided places for those referred by the courts as a condition of probation or a supervision order.

The Working Group recognized that motor projects can be useful in the diversion of young offenders from committing further offences but found that referral to a project was generally used as a last resort to avoid a lengthy custodial sentence.

They felt the development of many of the motor projects which cater for offenders referred from the courts as a condition of a probation order reflected, in part, the concern and desire of the courts to have sentencing disposals which are not just an alternative to custody but which also seek to engage actively with offenders and attempt to channel their energies from illegal motoring activities. They addressed the criticism that motor projects may be seen as a 'reward' for offending, expressing the opinion that referral to a motor project would be seen less as a reward if access to driving were part of a comprehensive range of educational and recreational activities that were open to a much wider range of 'at risk' young people, not just to those who are convicted of car crimes.

Briggs (1991) is a strong advocate of motor projects and believes that motor projects have much to offer in terms of rehabilitating young offenders where custodial sentences have failed. In his view, custodial sentences are generally ineffective in terms of deterrent and rehabilitation standards. He concludes that young people need programmes that deal with them on a personal basis, channel their energies positively and rebuild their confidence.

In South Wales, a motor project is in operation in Swansea (Guiding Hand), and at the time of writing, another project in South Glamorgan (Dragon Wheels) is about to become operational. The latter project will initially be for community sentences but will eventually also have a crime prevention focus and be open to all young people via youth clubs and schools. Guiding Hand is a registered charity, established in 1984. The committee has members from both statutory agencies and the voluntary sector. At present, the Project is for offenders only. An evaluation of the Project was carried out in 1992. The evaluation report stated that:

39% of the sample investigated had not re-offended whilst on the Project;

the types of young people who benefited most from the Project were those interested not only in driving but also in the mechanics of cars or motor cycles;

parents and relatives of offenders were unanimous in their belief that the Project is helping to reduce and stop offending;

referring agencies are convinced that the Project is a positive step to providing an alternative to custody;

offenders themselves are enthusiastic about the whole programme and are putting forward ideas of their own as to how it can be improved;

staff at the Project have created a working atmosphere which helps clients to come to terms with their offending and teaches them to function in a social environment;

the Project is achieving its aim and offering a realistic alternative to sentencing.

Views of police officers and social workers
Police officers and social workers interviewed for this study were asked for their opinions on motor projects, based on their experience. The police officers had mixed views. One officer felt they were good provided they were properly supervized; this point was emphasized by another officer, who felt they could become "a learning area to make them [young offenders] more advanced in the ways of crime".

In principle, the social workers interviewed were in favour of motor projects, seeing them as constructive schemes which young people could feel part of and thereby gain a measure of self-esteem. Some concerns were expressed, however, including the poor public perception of projects. Two workers questioned whether young people get enough excitement from racing around a track. The social workers were also of the opinion that projects should be for the use of the whole community and recommended that they should be set up in schools and youth clubs and linked to a central facility, such as a track. They felt that good funding was needed in order to run projects properly and that there could be difficulties in gatekeeping. Most were of the opinion that early intervention was required to prevent young people from becoming involved in crime.

Towards an ideal model

If set up with clear aims and objectives and sufficiently resourced, motor projects can offer a way of dealing with a young person 'obsession' with cars in a controlled way, while also working with the issue of their offending. In suggesting possible ways forward for the Mid Glamorgan multi-agency car crime strategy, The Children's Society collated a series of recommendations for the aims and management of motor projects. These were drawn from existing surveys of projects carried out by the Home Office, the South Wales Police and Leicester Action for Youth Trust.

In 1988, the Home Office Working Group on car crime made the following recommendations on motor projects:

> (1) increased community involvement (by local authorities, the police, schools and the business sector) in the development of motor projects which provide young people with access to driving and education in safe driving and social awareness and responsibility.

> (2) greater use by the courts of probation and supervision orders which require attendance at a motor project but not for the first offence.

> (3) there should be, where it is not already within the programmes of motor projects, emphasis upon the questions of morality, social awareness and concern for the victim of the offence.

(4) the use of cautions, where appropriate, which encourage attendance at a motor project. They stressed the need to avoid heavy and lightly convicted offenders mixing in the same project at the same time.

They also identified the need for a multi-agency approach for diverting young people away from car crime.

A South Wales police report of the Auto-Related Crime Working Group set out the aims a motor project should have:

(1) provision of opportunity for young people of all backgrounds to be introduced to projects where their interest can be directed into positive channels.

(2) advance education and training of young people under 25 years of age who have committed motor-related offences or whose circumstances suggest they are likely to commit such an offence.

(3) to encourage a positive interest in motor vehicles.

(4) to provide specific training in all aspects of motor mechanics, safety and handling.

(5) to develop social skills, powers of communication, community awareness and community involvement.

(6) to use all of the above to help the maturing process of young people in question and more fully equip them to be able to take a useful and responsible place in the community.

They recommended that projects should have a management committee, full-time staff to ensure continuity and a professional service delivery. They also felt that consideration should be given to secondment from main agencies for the full-time staffing cover of the project.

Moore and Lloyd (1992), who are part of Leicester Action for Youth Trust, suggested a particular direction for motor projects. They felt that motor projects were an answer to car crime as they 'offer the only realistic strategy for treating motor crime'. They felt that they offered some vulnerable young people in trouble the opportunities and relationships which could increase their self-esteem and have an impact on their offending.

Moore and Lloyd advocate a number of shifts in motor projects:

(1) Greater emphasis on road driving skills, maintaining the thrills but putting them in pespective.

(2) A move away from solely banger racing to a wider range of activity including motor bikes, go-carts, radio controlled cars and hovercraft.

(3) From open house to the use of programming and sessions within the project.

(4) Ensuring the projects have some educational content, even if informal.

(5) Improvements in referral and assessment procedures, therefore greater programming and targeting.

(6) Improvements in record-keeping and presentation of information about motor projects.

(7) Greater contact and collaboration with other organizations.

Initiatives designed to reduce the opportunity for car crime

There have been several moves in recent years to respond to the problem of increasing levels of car crime by improving the security of cars.

In 1985, the Home Office Standing Conference on Crime Prevention set up a Working Group on car security. They made a number of recommendations encouraging manufacturers to make car security a higher priority. They also recommended that car insurers should reflect in the cost of their premiums the presence or absence of sophisticated security devices.

In 1988, a second Working Group set up by the Home Office Standing Conference reported on car crime (and see previous chapter). Their main recommendations were: to study car crime prevention measures adopted in other countries; to ensure the production of a car crime prevention video for use in schools; and to encourage the development of a national programme along the lines of the Duke of Edinburgh's Award Scheme, which would provide young people with sufficient status to prevent them being drawn into a car crime sub-group.

The Working Group felt strongly that society and in particular the media should not trivialize car theft and recommended that the media should take action to de-glamorize car crime. They also endorsed recommendations made by the Working Group on car security that a car crime security campaign should be mounted and that manufacturers should introduce better security features.

Since the publication of the Report of the Working Group on car crime, a video has been produced by the Association of British Insurers called *Think Again*. A number of other videos have also been made by individual motor projects and remand centres as part of their education programmes.

What can be done?

Car Crime Prevention Year
In 1992, the Government launched Car Crime Prevention Year, a national advertizing campaign costing £5 million. For the purposes of this research, police officers and social workers were asked for their opinions on the campaign.

The police expressed mixed views. Some felt it was excellent (although most disliked the hyena logo used) and suggested it should be continued. One was of the opinion that "anything to assist in the epidemic" was welcome. Another felt that further commitment by the Government was needed and long overdue.

Most of the social workers were sceptical about the campaign. They did feel that it highlighted the individual's responsibility to ensure their car was secure but they felt that the increase in insurance premiums were equally effective in making the same point. They saw it as having little overall effect in curbing the problem of car crime.

Individual responsibility for car security
Official figures published by the Home Office show that 30% of people forget to lock their cars and 70% of all cars parked on the street have no security device fitted. Now that the security of cars forms an important part of evaluating an insurance risk, insurance companies are persuading individuals to be more conscious of their car's security.

Manufacturers' responsibility for car security
A *Which?* report (1991) examined the risk of car break-ins. It illustrated the reticence of some manufacturers to provide better security, seeing it as making the cars uncompetitively expensive.

> *"Customers want to spend hundreds of pounds on stereos and sun roofs but begrudge spending on an alarm to secure their vehicle."*
> Society of Motor Manufacturers and Traders

The 1988 British Crime Survey found, however, that nearly two-thirds of people would be prepared to pay extra for a comprehensive car security system.

A few manufacturers at the time of the *Which?* report were beginning to recognize that security was important and even a selling point: Vauxhall had fitted deadlocks and an alarm on some cars; Ford's Escort and Orion ranges had an alarm fitted as standard; some others, including Rover, also fitted alarms to their prestige ranges.

Which? tested several types of cars to determine how easy they were to break into. Most of the models held out for no longer than ten seconds and often less. They gave an overall score of 1 - 10: the higher the score, the more difficult the car was to break into.

The highest scoring cars were:

VW Passat CL	10
Vauxhall Carlton Estate	7

The cars most commonly taken in Mid Glamorgan — Vauxhall Astras, Cavaliers and Ford Escorts and Fiestas — all had a below-average score of 3.

Which? concluded that car manufacturers needed to make sure that all their cars met the British Standards for security and that they should all be fitted with alarms, preferably as standard equipment but, failing that, as an optional extra. They also advised that models that were easier to break into should be shunned by car buyers.

Practical security measures - an evaluation
Gow and Peggrem (1991) found that *security etching* (having the registration number etched onto the car window and elsewhere on the car) had little effect, as cars were commonly 'borrowed' rather than intended for long-term use. They also advocated *improved lighting in car parks*.

The Home Office Car Theft Index
The first Home Office Car Theft Index for England and Wales was published in 1992. By recording details of each vehicle stolen, the Index shows the rate at which any given model of car is stolen over a one-year period. The method of calculation allows for the fact that certain makes/models are far more numerous than others and, therefore, far more likely to be stolen.

The Index is important for both car owners and manufacturers. It tells existing car owners which cars are more likely to be stolen and allows car manufacturers to monitor the success or failure of crime prevention measures.

The 1992 Index showed that more than half a million cars were stolen in England and Wales in the previous year. The likeliest cars to be stolen came from a small 'high risk' category. They included Escorts, Sierras and Vauxhall Astras. On average, 6% of the high risk band are stolen every year. The low risk band, which includes Citroëns and Ladas, had an average of 0.7% theft.

The Car Theft Index concluded that:

- the majority of car thefts tended to be concentrated on relatively few model ranges;
- a risk of theft for a car from a high risk category may be up to four times greater than that of other cars;
- high performance cars are three times more likely to be stolen than low performance cars (some high performance cars are ten times more likely to be stolen);
- many high risk cars tend to be older, from the late 1970s and early 1980s.

Among the reasons given for this last conclusion were that older cars tended to be parked in poorer, high risk areas; owners did not bother with security because they did not believe it to be worthwhile; and the manufacturor-installed security systems of many older cars were inadequate.

Vehicle Watch Scheme

Vehicle Watch was introduced to South Wales in 1990, following the apparent success of similar Schemes in other parts of Britain. Membership of the Scheme is free. Members display a sticker on their windscreens, which is intended as a deterrent to thieves. Cars displaying these stickers are more likely to be stopped by the police between midnight and 5am. Certain insurance companies also offer discounts to drivers who are members of Vehicle Watch.

An article in the *Western Mail* in Spring, 1992, stated:

> *"Police throughout Wales have described the initiative as one of the most successful anti-crime schemes they have undertaken. 'From the statistics, we know that a car carrying the Vehicle Watch Sticker is 12 times less likely to be stolen or broken into than a car without one,' said a spokesman."*

Honess and Maguire (1993) were, however, less optimistic about the success of the Scheme. Their objective was to evaluate the impact of Vehicle Watch upon the problem of car theft in Gwent. They looked at crime statistics, Vehicle Watch membership data and carried out a street and postal survey and interviews with the public and police.

They found that members of Vehicle Watch were significantly less likely than non-members to have their cars stolen. Only 11% of the victims of car theft in Gwent were members of Vehicle Watch. However, they suggested that the difference in victimization rates of members and non-members may be due to other factors. For example, those who join Vehicle Watch tend to be more 'security conscious' than the average car owner; they also tend to own types of cars less likely to be stolen and to keep or park their cars in safer locations.

Honess and Maguire did find that the Scheme had a favourable image with the public and so was successful in reducing some of the fear of car theft. Almost one-quarter of those interviewed said they felt 'much more secure' about their car as a result of joining and 46% 'a little more secure'. There seemed to be no widespread belief, however, that the Scheme improved the chances of car thieves being either deterred or detected. The authors found that some public confidence in the Scheme was lost through the 'apparent failure of police officers to stop and check cars as often as members were led to believe'. Honess and Maguire conclude:

> *"While Vehicle Watch may have a temporary effect on car theft rates in areas with high publicity and high take up rates for the Scheme, the case is by no means a strong one."*

Our findings support this view: comments on page 40 illustrate that the Scheme appears to have little effect as a deterrent with the young people interviewed.

Media coverage

Media coverage of car crime involving young people has a powerful influence and deserves special mention. There is no doubt that the media have a difficult job in trying to report car crime responsibly and in a balanced way. It is unfortunate that certain sectors of the media have chosen to opt for sensationalism rather than more balanced reporting. Sadly, headlines such as these have become all too common over the last few years:

'Murderous' joyriders sentenced to custody

Joyriders run riot in Wales

TWO POLICE cars were rammed as joyriders went on a "murderous" driving spree at speeds of more than 110mph, a court heard yesterday.

TEENAGE CAR thieves are running riot in South Wales.

Death-car drinkers will face

What can be done?

As part of the interviews for this research, both the social workers and the police officers were asked for their views on how the media covered the problem of car crime.

Both police officers and social workers were concerned about car crime being portrayed as 'exciting' and encouraging 'copy cat' offences. One police officer felt there should be no video footage car chases and more concentration on the fatal consequences. Another officer saw the press as lacking sensitivity and another felt that the media should not persist in calling it 'joyriding.'

One social worker was concerned about the recent publicity covering 'ram-raiding' (when a car is used to 'ram' a shop window to gain access), believing that the television coverage may have encouraged others to try it out.

As stated on page 57, the Home Office Working Group on car crime recommended in 1988 that the media de-glamorize car crime, believing that car theft should not be trivialized. The press in their own style have begun to do this. In some instances, however, newspapers have attempted to run campaigns to 'stop the joyriders' by singling out specific offenders. These methods are counter-productive, individualizing the crimes and encouraging specific young people to live up to their media image.

The media is a powerful and persuasive influence upon young people and one that plays a large part in creating their expectations. High performance cars, so the manufacturers would like the public to believe, are a symbol of success, power and sexual potency. This is the image which is constantly presented to young people and one which they may be seeking to attain, albeit illegally.

The media may have attempted to de-glamorize the theft but they have not yet begun to try to de-glamorize the allure of the high performance car.

CONCLUSION

Our review of the available evidence concerning some of the more innovative responses to car crime suggested a number of ways forward. Taken together with the themes that emerged from our interviews with young offenders, we identified a range of proposals for the Mid Glamorgan Working Party on Car Crime to consider when outlining their Strategy.

The proposals focused in particular on:

* preventive measures designed to reduce the opportunity for car crime;

* educative programmes which aim to deter young people from car crime;

* responses to known offenders.

It was recommended that any new developments should be rigorously monitored and evaluated to assess their impact on car crime in the local area. Part Four presents details of the developments in Mid Glamorgan to which this research contributed, together with conclusions and recommendations arising from this study.

PART IV

A WAY FORWARD

Developments within Mid Glamorgan

by Howell Edwards, Principal Officer, Mid
Glamorgan Social Services

As described on pages 2 - 4, the Mid Glamorgan Car Crime Working
Party was set up in November 1990. The Children's Society's research,
on which the current report is based, has been crucial in informing the
work of this group.

In addition, information has been collated from a number of other
Sources:

a wide range of motor projects in England and Wales;

the School Liaison Service of the South Wales Police;

current work with car crime offenders by the Social
Services Department and the Probation Service.

The result of the deliberations of the Working Party was the publication of
the Strategy to combat car crime, which has been widely circulated and
endorsed by the statutory agencies and the Mid Glamorgan County
Council.

The conclusions were as follows:

1. The level of car crime within the county was a cause of much concern; it necessitated a Mid Glamorgan Car Crime Strategy to be adopted by all the appropriate agencies. The Strategy should include the following elements:

> crime prevention services
> education programmes
> programmes of work with young offenders

2. In order to have any positive impact on young people convicted of, or thought to be involved in taking vehicle's without the owner's consent, opportunity has to be made available for them to drive cars in an environment which is safe both for themselves and for others, but which offers elements of danger and excitement. Such opportunities will need to establish an assessment criteria to ensure that such schemes are appropriately targeted.

3. Any motor project established should be made available to young people generally and should not be solely for young offenders. It is acknowledged that projects may need to organize separate opportunities for these young people.

4. The impact and long-term viability of motor projects is substantially enhanced by being community based. Every effort should thus be made to involve community groups in the establishing of any such projects.

5. Though many motor projects were said to be successful, there is a clear need to generate evidence as to the effectiveness or otherwise of motor projects in reducing the re-offending levels of those who attend. Any motor project established should therefore be closely monitored and evaluated by an independent organization.

6. The most effective motor projects have been those where there has been a considerable amount of collaboration and partnership between the various statutory agencies. Inter-agency support to the motor projects should be thus seen as being of fundamental importance, both in terms of establishing the projects and in ensuring their long-term viability.

Current developments

In order to assist in the implementation of the strategic plan, the Social Services Department is appointing an Auto-Crime Development Worker, whose main responsibility will be to bring into existence local voluntary-run motor projects.

The County Working Group has continued to act in a co-ordinating role and is encouraging the development of local workshops run by voluntary groups, with a view to utilising the Dragon Wheels track based in Cardiff for the actual driving of the banger cars.

Within the six Districts of Mid Glamorgan, there are currently several developments underway. In one District, a group comprised of representatives from the statutory agencies, the voluntary sector and the local business community are forming themselves into a company limited by guarantee, and applying for charitable status. Some funding has already been received from the Probation Service and it is hoped that premises equipment and staffing will be available by April 1994 in order for the project to become operational.

In another District, a development is based on an existing well-established voluntary project. Using existing garage facilities within the Project, and with some funding already having been received from a variety of sources, it is anticipated that the motor project will be taking referrals during Autumn 1993, and be open to offenders and non-offenders.

Discussions are also taking place in a third District with interested organizations, with a view to establishing a motor project in that area. There is also interest within the County of establishing a scheme based on motorcycles, as in some areas this has proved to be an effective way of diverting some young people away from car crime.

As it is the intention that the impact of these initiatives be evaluated for their effectiveness in reducing car crime, discussions are underway with an interested local university, with a view to them establishing and undertaking the research and monitoring.

The situation in Mid Glamorgan is at an exciting stage. With the appointment of the County Development Worker, coupled with the local initiatives, the time when each of the six Districts within the Authority has access to a motor project may not be too far in the future. One can only then hope that real inroads will then be made into reducing the very high levels of car crime that occur in Mid Glamorgan.

Conclusions and recommendations

The problem of car crime is a complex one and there is no simple and absolute solution. The responsibility for dealing with it belongs to all agencies and a successful car crime strategy needs, in the first instance, a multi-agency approach that involves the local community.

The contributory factors of crime over and above the individual's motivation are many and complicated. The effects of the current recession, with increased unemployment, cannot be ignored. The young people of Mid Glamorgan who took part in this research were, on the whole, young people who felt they had no future, no hope and certainly nothing to aim for. Perhaps that lack of hope manifests itself in crime and particularly in car crime which provides disaffected young people with an opportunity to 'succeed'. Stealing cars, driving at high speeds and initiating 'chases' involves a fair degree of skill and daring which are fully appreciated by the offender's peer group. Our respondents demonstrated that the group nature of much car crime among young people is a powerful factor in sustaining the individual's offending behaviour, even, at times, following serious accidents.

Some young offenders said they committed car theft out of boredom. There was a belief amongst both the professionals and young people interviewed that young people would 'grow out of it', as they matured and became responsible. Most inevitably do — Home Office statistics indicate that 75% of those found guilty or cautioned for car crime in 1989 were under 21 years of age. But there is a clear need for diversionary strategies to assist young people through the vulnerable years, in the form of improved leisure facilities and increased training and job opportunities.

Car crime strategy

Our findings suggest that the focus of consideration for an multi-agency strategy aimed at combatting car crime amongst young people, should be around two broad categories:

* Responses to offending behaviour
* Crime prevention

Responses to offending behaviour

Most of the young people interviewed said one of their main motivations for taking cars was their attraction to driving. Many young people commit car crime for the 'fun' or 'buzz'. It has been described by some young people and by social workers as 'an addiction'. Initiatives targeting those who have already been identified as offenders must take cognizance of what their offending activities offer them: a mixture of status, excitement and self-esteem. Responses will have to provide comparable rewards if they are to maintain offenders on programme.

Provision of a legitimate outlet for an interest in driving and cars

Responses must also treat the group nature of car crime with the potency it deserves. Most of the young offenders interviewed for the study had met other car thieves whilst they were accommodated by the local authority. The wisdom of placing young offenders in institutions and thereby providing them with opportunities to share crime-related knowledge, is thus shown to be highly questionable.

In order for young people to be deterred from the need to steal cars, it is thus important that they are provided with the opportunity to obtain a comparable 'buzz' within a safe environment. Motor projects can provide such opportunities and have demonstrated some success in reducing re–offending amongst known offenders. Figures quoted by NAMP are impressive:

> *"Eight out of ten sent to prison for auto crime re-offended within two years. Seven out of ten who stay with a motor project for over three months do not re-offend within two years."*

If motor projects are to be enabled to work with young offenders, the confidence of the court has to be gained.

Motor projects have been criticized as providing 'rewards' for offending behaviour. In cases where scheme are made available to all young people, however, a positive and preventive image is presented to young people, funders and the community at large.

Crime prevention

The term 'crime prevention' is used to describe initiatives designed to deter young offenders through educative programmes, presenting a less attractive image of car crime. It also encompasses measures to make the stealing of cars more difficult. The recommendations listed below offer ways forward for a series of initiatives which may be developed by a multi-agency strategy on car crime.

Education
Both the social workers and police officers interviewed felt there should be more crime prevention education both at school and at youth clubs, which stressed the dangers of car crime.

Evidence shows that children under 14 years old are already 'being carried' in car theft incidents. In order to prevent younger children from succumbing to peer pressure and becoming involved in car crime, prevention programmes should be targeted at this age range.

The responses from young people suggested that it would be effective to involve ex-offenders in these educative programmes.

The Media
The media are in a strong position to illustrate the seriousness of car crime. The Home Office Working Party recommended in 1988 that the media should adopt strategies to de-glamorize car crime. Although the advertising campaign accompanying the Government's Crime Prevention Year 1992 was an attempt to do this, sensationalized accounts of car crime and profiles of young people involved are still common.

Improved security measures
The opportunistic nature of car crime committed by young people suggests there is considerable scope for improving security measures. Such measures fall into three broad areas of responsibility:

Personal
All car owners and drivers can make a significant contribution to improved security. Putting cars in garages or behind locked gates in a driveway at night, if possible, is one simple but effective measure.

73

Car Manufacturers

Car manufacturers are beginning to listen to the demand for increased security, but there is still scope for further improvements.

Local Authority

Street lighting, security in car parks and other measures can make stealing cars more difficult and no longer an opportunistic 'pastime'. A recent voucher parking scheme introduced in Cardiff city centre is reported to have reduced car crime in the area since its introduction 12 months ago. The Western Mail reported in September 1993 that the increased surveillance provided by the additional 19 traffic wardens deployed to assist in the enforcement of the scheme, had 'warned off' potential car theives.

RECOMMENDATIONS:

(1) that access to driving be provided prior to the age of 17 at school, in youth clubs and in motor projects.

(2) that in order to obtain maximum success, motor projects involve representatives from all agencies working with young offenders: the police, social services, probation, magistrates, and the wider community.

(3) that motor projects be developed as a resource for all young people and not only known offenders.

(4) a multi-agency car crime strategy should include:

(i) programmes designed to educate young people as to the dangers of car crime, where possible involving ex-offenders for maximum effect, should be introduced into all secondary schools. Families, schools, youth clubs and other community institutions should be encouraged to assist boys and young men in challenging the powerful stereotype that associates driving fast cars with manhood.

(ii) a media campaign: local newspapers, radio and TV stations should be contacted and educated in presenting more balanced and responsible reports of car crime incidents.

(iii) strategies for raising public awareness of car security issues. These should include a) personal security measures; b) security devices fitted to cars by manufacturers; c) local authority reviews of street lighting, security in car parks and traffic surveillance.

Appendix One

PREVIOUS RESEARCH
In Britain numerous studies about car theft have appeared in criminology journals over the last four decades. It has been an area of concern since the 1950s and has been described by various sectors as a 'cult'. The term 'joyriding' was probably used first by the media. Although its origin is uncertain, it may have been so called because cars were not taken for material gain but for fun. It is certainly a term which is used more by the media and general public than by the offenders or the police.

W.G. McCarney (1981) looked at the cult of joyriding in West Belfast, where boys stole cars and tempted the police to chase them. The study looked at the underlying motives and the part played by fear and courage.

Howard Parker (1984) notes the persistence of joyriding as a delinquent activity in Merseyside despite a number of fatalities and punitive sentencing by the courts. Parker outlines the pattern of car theft. Initially, he writes, young people try to open car doors, sometimes stealing items from inside, and move on to learning the techniques of how to break in and start cars either by trial and error or from other young people. Eventually cars are driven and joyriding begins. The numbers involved begins to spread as the idea that it is exciting is passed on to others. Then, for some, there may be an ambition to move on from cars that are easy to get into and start to higher-status faster cars. There may also be a move to driving further away from the immediate neighbourhood to increase the chances of being spotted by the police and chased. Parker stresses the potential rewards of joyriding for young people in terms of action, excitement, status, prestige, and aspiring to (or wanting to destroy) the symbol of success and respectability which other people have.

This idea is pursued by **Rod Moore** (1990) who refers to Parker's finding that it offers young people action and status. Moore discusses the role of crime prevention strategies and underlines the need for youth workers to stay in touch with the changing needs of young people and examine the potential of cars as a medium for social education and learning.

Greater Manchester Probation Service (1990) carried out a survey into car crime. The results were from a questionnaire completed by 86 offenders, all male, aged between 14 and 26.

They found that certain cars such as sporty models, expensive ones and those not locked were targeted. The most common way of entering was to force or break the lock. Car crime was carried out as a group activity with the main motivations being for money, excitement, or to drive. When asked whether driving a go-cart on a track would give them the same sort of buzz, 34% said yes, 51% said no.

A more local study (unpublished) was carried out by the **Barnardo's 175 Project** (1991) in Newport. The survey used a questionnaire completed by 50 young people already involved in Juvenile Justice Programmes. The 175 Project has a TWOC programme involving go-cart racing, visits to a hospital, talks with the police and offending counselling.

The study found that cars were stolen mainly from car parks in the late evening or early hours of the morning. Offences were committed on impulse but high performance cars would be targeted. The preferred way of entering was by breaking a window or forcing a lock, which most had learnt from friends or from custody or care. Car alarms were only a partial deterrent and then only the most sophisticated models. The motivation was mainly the excitement, with theft from cars being an opportunist consequence. Chases by the police were encouraged.

The report concluded that there was evidence of a shared knowledge of car theft among the young people. The stimulus received was very high and they believed it gave the offender status amongst his peers. They saw it as a highly visible offence which could be motivated by an anti-authoritarian outlook in addition to the excitement factor.

Jeff Briggs (1991) aimed to identify the factors which caused young people to joyride and assess the effectiveness of motor projects.

Briggs interviewed 30 subjects aged between 11 and 17 who had been convicted of TWOC. He found that most young people planned to go out and take cars, looking for high performance models and ones which were easy to enter with no security devices. The main reasons they gave for taking cars were: the need to impress others; to feel important; for fun; and to relieve boredom. Doing it to make money scored low. Half admitted to inciting chases from the police. When asked if being involved in a motor project would stop them taking cars illegally, 90% said yes.

Light, Nee and Ingham (1993) carried out interviews with a sample of one hundred car crime offenders aged between 14 and 35 years old. They found that most of those interviewed said they began to steal cars in their early to mid teens, with the help of more experienced offenders. They identified the main reasons for first getting involved as peer pressure, boredom and excitement. The excitement of car theft seemed to overcome any worry of the threat of punishment. The study found that after a time, making money from taking cars became more important with over one-third of respondents progressing to 'professional' car theft for financial gain. Most of those who said they had stopped taking cars put this down to maturity. They regarded penal sanctions as relatively unimportant in stopping offending.

All these studies have contributed to the understanding of car crime and have shown that it is mainly a group activity with a sub-culture of its own, carried out for the excitement rather than monetary gain. Unfortunately, this also makes it one of the most difficult problems to tackle.

Appendix Two

THE LAW RELATING TO THEFT AND CARS

Offence	Act	Maximum penalty fine/imprisonment
Theft of a motor vehicle	Theft Act 1968 S1	£2000 6 months
Attempted theft of a motor vehicle	Criminal attempts Act 1981 S9	£1000 3 months
Taking without owner's consent	Theft Act 1968 S12	£2000 6 months
Attempted TWOC	Criminal Attempts Act 1981 S9	£1000 3 months
Going equipped to steal	Theft Act 1968 S25	£2000 6 months
Tampering (vehicle interference)	Criminal Attempts Act 1981 S9	£1000 3 months
Allow to be carried	Theft Act 1968 S12	£2000 6 months
Theft from a motor vehicle	Criminal Attempts Act 1981 S9	£1000 3 months
Taking a vehicle driving dangerously, causing injury, death or damage	Aggravated Vehicle Taking Act 1992	Unlimited fine 2 years (5 if death caused) automatic driving ban

Notes

Road Traffic Act covers offences such as driving without a licence, whilst disqualified or without insurance are not covered.

Disqualification from driving can be a mandatory or discretionary penalty depending on the offence.

Compensation can be ordered either as part of a wider sentence or, in some cases, by itself as a penalty. If the offender's means are limited priority will be given to compensation if appropriate rather than a fine.

78

Appendix Three

QUESTIONS FOR SEMI-STRUCTURED INTERVIEWS
WITH YOUNG PEOPLE

(1) BACKGROUND
1. How old were you when you got involved with taking cars for the first time ?
2. How old are you now ?
3. Can you make a guess at how many cars you've taken during that time ?
4. The first time you were involved with taking a car, can you tell me what happened ?
5. How did you learn to get into them ?
6. How did you learn to drive ?

(2) SUB-CULTURE
7. Do you have family or friends who take cars ?
8. Did you take cars on your own or with someone else ?
9. What would you say made you decide to take a car at any time ? Can you describe a typical time ?
10. Used you to go out planning to take a car ?
11. Did you ever show anyone else how to take cars ?

(3) METHOD
12. How did you normally get into a car ?
13. How long did it take ?
14. How did you start the car ?

(4) TYPES OF CAR
15. Did you take any type of car ?
16. Which cars are the easiest to take ?
17. Which cars would you not take ?
18. Which cars are the most difficult to take ?
19. What is your favourite type of car ?

(5) PRACTICAL FACTORS
20. Used you to take cars at any particular time of day or night ?
21. Was there any particular area or place you would take them from ?

(6) DRIVING SKILLS
22. Have you ever had an accident in a car you have taken ?
23. What was the fastest speed you have ever done in a car you have taken ?
24. Have you ever read the highway code ?

(7) DETERRENTS
25. If you owned a car,how would you stop it being taken ?
26. Did you ever take a car which had a car alarm ?
27. Was there anything which ever stopped you taking a car ?
28. Have you ever seen a Vehicle Watch sticker ? What do you think about them ?
29. If you have stopped taking cars, what made you stop ? What would make you stop taking cars ?

(8) SELF - IMAGE
30. If you owned a car which was stolen, what would you think about the person who took it ?
31. How would you rate yourself as a driver ?

(9) CONSEQUENCES
32. When you took a car,did you ever think about getting caught ?
33. What did you think about the police ?
34. What did you think about the owner of the car ?
35. Did you ever think about having an accident ?
36. Did you ever think about being disqualified from driving if you got caught ?
37. Were you ever chased by the police in a car ? Did that happen often ?

(10) MOTIVATION
38. What reasons would you give for why you took cars ?
39. What was the best thing about taking cars ?
40. Had you ever been drinking or taking drugs when you took cars ?

(11) ASSOCIATED CRIME
41. Did you ever take anything from a car you had stolen ?
42. Were you ever asked by anybody else to take cars? For what reason ?
43. Did you ever damage the car after you had finished with it ? Why ?

Bibliography

Aggravated Vehicle Taking Act 1992 HMSO

Briggs, J. (1991) *A Profile of a Juvenile Joyrider* University of Durham

Carr, A.P. (1992) *Anthony and Berryman's Magistrates' Court Guide* Butterworths

Crime, Alcohol, Drugs and Leisure (1992) *A Survey of 13,437 Young People at School in Mid Glamorgan* Unpublished: Mid Glamorgan Social Crime Prevention Unit

Gow, J. and Peggram, A. (1991) *Car Crime Culture? A Study of Motor Vehicle Theft by Juveniles* Unpublished survey: Barnardo's 175 Project, Newport

Guiding Hand Motor Project (1992) *An Evaluation* Unpublished: West Glamorgan Crime Prevention Initiative

Home Office Standing Conference on Crime Prevention (1985) *Report of the Working Group on Car Security* Home Office

Home Office Standing Conference on Crime Prevention (1988) *Report of the Working Group on Car Crime* Home Office

Home Office Statistical Bulletin (April 1991 to March 1992) *Notifiable Offences* Home Office

Honess, T. and Maguire, M. (1993) *Vehicle Watch and Car Theft: An Evaluation* Police Research Group Paper HMSO

Houghton, G. (1992) *Car Theft in England and Wales: The Home Office Car Theft Index* CPU Paper 33 Home Office

Isles, E. (1992) *An Examination of Sentencing Trends in the Use of Custodial Sentences and Supervision Orders in the Courts of West Glamorgan 1989–1991* West Glamorgan Social Services Department

Light, R., Nee, C. and Ingham, H. (1993) *Car Theft: The Offenders' Perspective* HMSO

McCarney, W.G (1981) J*oyriding: A Quest for Identity* Youth in Society

Bibliography

Moore, R. (1990) *Taken for a Ride: Joyriding in the 90's* Youth Clubs with the Edge

Moore, R. and Lloyd, G. (1992) *Looking Beyond Banger Racing* Youth Social Work

Moore, T.G. (1990) *Taking Without Consent: An Accelerating Problem* Justice of the Peace

Oxford Police Area Commander Report 1991

Parker, H. (1984) *Locking Up the Joyriders* Youth in Society

Peters, C. (1992) *Youth Driver Education - A Role for the Youth & Community* Young People Now

South Wales Constabulary *Annual Report* 1991

Thames Valley Police Report 1992

Which? *Cars at Risk* Which? February 1991

The Advocacy Unit – Wales

The Children's Society's Advocacy Unit was established in 1989 in order to take forward the lessons learnt from the Society's experience of working with young people in trouble.

The Unit promotes effective youth justice strategies in Wales to limit the numbers of young people entering custody and residential care.

We also seek to ensure that those young people who are locked away are in childcare establishments rather than penal custody.

In pursuit of our objectives we undertake

- Training, consultancy and a comprehensive information service.
- Review, monitoring, and evaluation of the effectiveness of services for young offenders.
- Enhancing public understanding of young people in society, particularly young people in trouble.

Recent work

- Contributing to the review of secure care in Wales.
- Developing strategies and targeted responses to replace remands to custody.
- Advice and information services for young people sentenced to long terms of detention.
- Research and publications on car crime amongst young people.
- Development of children's rights initiatives with local authority partners.

The Children's Society
The Children's Society is a national voluntary organization of the
Church of England and the Church in Wales. It exists to work for child-
ren and young people, irrespective of their race or religious belief:

- to help them grow in their families and communites
- to help them take charge of their own lives
- to help them change the conditions that stand in their way.

The Children's Society runs 126 projects throughout England and Wales
including:

- working with young offenders, offering them a constructive alternative to crime
- providing independent living units for young people leaving care
- working with young people living on the street
- family centres and neighbourhood groups in local communities
where families are under stress, often feeling isolated and powerless to
improve their lives
- residential and day care for children and young people with disabilities
- helping children and young people with special needs to find new
families
- offering independent guardian ad litems for children involved in care
proceedings
- promoting the rights of children and young people.

The Children's Society is committed to raising public awareness of
issues affecting childen and young people and to promoting their welfare and rights in matters of public policy. The Society produces a wide
range of publications, including reports, briefing papers and educational
material.

For further information about the work of The Children's Society or to
obtain a full publications list, please contact:

The Publications Department
The Children's Society
Edward Rudolf House
Margery Street
London
WC1X 0JL   tel 071-837 4299; fax 071-837 0211